Deep Unto Deep

David Hodges

Deep Unto Deep

ISBN 9780956688446
Acknowledgements
Spirituality, The Furrow, Theology,
The Merton Journal and The Merton Seasonal
in which some of these poems first appeared

Published by The Abbey, Caldey Island,
Tenby, Pembs. SA70 7UH, Wales, G.B.

Table of content

Deep Unto Deep

Below the far horizon
the sun slowly sinks.
On the world's edge,
the sea is deeper than thought.
Breathing in the ocean breeze,
I watch the movement of the waves,
the waves that lead to you;
a silence too full of meaning for words.

Endless stars light the clear night,
a night opening out more and more,
alive with mysterious life;
deep calls to deep,
a night speaking of life without end,
of love beyond recall.

Dawn Prayer

In the quiet of dawn,
the moment intense but empty
as the lonely horizon;
the silent sea
calm and still, mirroring
the silence within.
Yet I feel absent from Him.

Then the remembered Word,
rising softly, nurses
my soul, held in God's love.
The moment continues
inside the mystery;
in silent awareness
there seems no end.

The Storm

Dark thunderclouds begin to fill
a sky of hazy blue,
the air has cooled from thick and sticky.
Birds stop singing to the morning,
tense for the flicker light,
the cracking open of the sky.

After the storm, the brief relief
of hissing rain, all is sharp and clear;
the smell of damp and settled dust,
and all around is dripping glad.
Birds begin to chase the air;
we're back again to endless summer.

Into the Deep

Such turmoil above,
such stillness below;
the stormy sea anchored
by its calm depth beneath.

After the storm,
the calm chant of the tide;
while all hope seemed lost,
down deep, my heart at peace.

Sandtop

Was it minutes, hours,
that afternoon?
I watched and watched
until the tide stood still.
Far out against the strand,
flocks of waders locked in time,
all movement subtle,
no breath of wind.

The sea merged with the sky;
cloud and sand and sea,
even the air was golden,
all normal rules suspended,
the moment eternal.
I slowly knelt
to catch it in a single frame.

A Place Remembered

In the pale remembered light,
just the sound
of the sea gently lapping.
The late evening sun
turning red in the west.

Our small lives uplifted,
rising far above what just before
hung heavy over us.
What silent joy,
what peace we found.

Caldey

Far from all
in the outside world,
seeming distant in time
as well as space;
a place where nature thrives,
a place where arum lilies
grow like weeds;
where the earth awakens
crisp and pure;
where all the outside world's allure
does not monastic peace disturb;
where solitude and silence speak
in the presence of the Word;
where God delights in giving,
bountiful and forgiving;
where God gives and waits,
our joyful, free response anticipates.

Caldey (2)

All life appears on hold,
the stone walls gapped,
most of the fields abandoned now.
Just the sound of the skylark
high in the sky,
until starlings swirl away
from hooves of galloping cobs,
like waves breaking
in the lonely bay.

St Margaret's Island

Looking across
the tidal causeway,
the rocky sea-gates
that separate two islands,
it's strange to see
my island so familiar,
yet from here enchanting.
It's strange to imagine
quarrying families here,
eking out a meagre living
divided by a quarry;
or yet much further back,
a cloistered group of nuns
relying on the Caldey monks
to bring Communion and supplies,
tide and weather permitting.
Now a sanctuary for birds,
a place to see the puffins
since the rats have gone.

The Warrior Returns

(for Br Paul*)

We heard distant reports
of the last battle you fought,
how you were 'bound and gagged'
and that your life ebbed away.

Our boat brought you back
in a coffin at dawn,
just the boat and the boatman,
a grey mist on the water.

We dug a grave in the rain,
paid our hasty respects,
remembered your life, final pains,
saw you off to join the elect.

There were not many who knew you,
too few to recall
the old stories you told
of past battles you fought.

You hid your life from view,
bearing the scars withal,
you smiled through it all,
your face told the story.

A rough diamond, strange beauty,
cut and shaped by your life,
to yourself you were true,
faith and hope shone through.

A bare cross marks your grave,
through cloud sun shines for the brave.
Your place empty in choir,
now you're gone to celestial fire.

Died in intensive care on the mainland

St Samson's Isle

Set here apart, our island home,
to be alone with the Alone,
a stepping-stone
to another world
more glorious than our own.

Why did you come?
What do you seek?
What otherness, what wilderness,
to tame the wildness
you find within?

What master do you serve?
You will find here
the One who came to serve,
to tame and shape your selfish heart
to turn to love of others.

To be crushed then healed,
a heart to open and dilate,
a heart to be fulfilled
in prayer, transforming humankind,
its loves, its evils and its hate.

You will seek in solitude
the hidden things of God,
to reach that inner harbour
where the love of God
will be your one desire.

In Church

All around,
the sound of the sea
and wind through trees.
In here, stone and air
hold my prayer,
protected by the shadows.
The Holy Spirit is the source,
directs the course;
the meaning held in silence,
attentive to a subtle music
that resonates within.

Night-Owl Lectio

On a cool dark night,
in soft moonlight,
across my open window
glides a ghostly shape,
luminous, floating forward
in the silent air,
face towards me, huge eyes
like moons, wide shining,
strangely knowing,
curious, interrupting
my encounter with the Word.
We see each other,
I just sitting with the text
at wisdom's feet.

Flying the Nest

Four raven chicks
readying for flight,
jet black, in their scraggy nest
tucked in a cleft
on Red Stack.

Above, the mother circling
with her loud, choked croak.
Father gliding, tumbling, diving,
giving an acrobatic display.
Huge beaks: all keep away.

Scavengers, fierce hunters,
but capable of wisdom and charity
as Elijah and St Benedict testify.
Yet Apollo punished them
and there are other, darker myths.

Soon the chicks will need to find
another island to survive.
Standing now, still some grace about them,
how quickly they will move from innocence
to strutting, brooding malevolence.

The Skylark

High, high in a cloudless sky,
spinning ever higher on the wing,
I heard my first skylark sing.
Looking up until he vanished,
stock still I felt the thrill,
my heart quite ravished,
not heeding time that passed.

When to earth at last
I saw him almost fall,
he seemed so small,
so dull and brown and clumsy.
It seemed so wrong,
such mismatch with the beauty
of his flight and song.

Hawk

Hawk against the wind,
dark clouds scudding;
grass, trees bending;
a thunder crack surprises,
the sound of rain rises.
Just the sound of falling water.

After rain, the air
now clean and fresh,
the bay drawn sharp and clear;
birds, small creatures stir.
The hawk appears, ripping the air,
resumes his usual business.

Dawn Prayer (2)

In the cool breeze
my morning prayer
enlivened by the Spirit

My heart awakened
like tall trees tipped with gold
in the dawning light

Morning Lectio

Put out into the deep,
pay out the net
of the Lord's word.
Let the mind be hungry,
the heart astir,
a pure vessel
for the catch.

St Agnes' Blood Moon*

After we had prayed St Agnes' Vigil
and all the night was cold and still,
with half the world in bed,
we saw the rare blood moon
and when the sun rose, soon
the sky was streaked with red.
We know our sins, though scarlet, shameful,
in Christ's blood will be white as wool.

St Agnes, not yet thirteen,
a chaste lamb, so pure, so keen
to witness to the love of Christ,
whose blood for her had paid the price,
was a martyr for the Son of God
in whose steps she trod,
refusing to deny him.
In her there was no sin,
for her it was no loss
to die for him
who died for her upon the Cross.

*Total lunar eclipse, with red light refracted
around the Earth and striking the Moon on
St Agnes' Day, 21st January, 2019

Prayer

Outside the day-to-day,
the hectic, empty race;
leaving behind
the weight of the past,
the future for a while on hold;
out of time, the mood
of the moment left behind.

The self now inside out,
absent to self
but present to the One;
bared and open to the light,
to healing and forgiveness.
Now on the path
to living in the One.

Prayer (2)

Let my prayer be bold
for my heart is cold.
To God I pray
to be more aware
of his tender care;
that he will this day
light up that spark
within my narrow heart,
create the space
for him to come.
I seek his face,
to see the glory of the One,
that seeing whom I love
and loving whom I see,
I may die to self
to live in Love Himself.

Fire Prayer

Frost fire glare,
wisps of red mist,
ice on the margins of the lakes,
the morning crisp and clear
with the purity of a child.

Red sunlight
floods the morning sky,
the ice-cold water bright,
twin lakes shining
like the eyes of a prophet.

Are you ready yet to burn,
become all flame,
your heart afire,
filled with love's desire
at the morning prayer?

Love

When you are kind
it is God I find;
into all you breathe his life,
the mouth of your tender
heart wide open.
God's love is written
on the pages of your heart.

You show the face of God to me,
yet you are so patient
in awaiting something from me,
somehow giving me the means
to respond in love
in a way for me surprising,
unexpected.

Grief

Your smile, your laughter
and your listening ear
alive still in the autumn air;
this souls' meeting sundered
when the pain of loss
begins to prick my heart.

Memories kept alive
at the cost of pain,
life breaks the reverie,
your face fragments
in scattering rain
upon the window pane.

Things left unfinished,
unforgiven, unresolved,
things regrettably not done,
love unexpressed, now you're gone:
too late. But imagine meeting,
forgiving from the heart.

In the ache, the agony,
the chaos of the loss,
the gnawing pain of separation,
a silent embrace, prayer brings relief,
journeying through grief
to a place of hope awakened.

Now in the music of all nature
your presence quickens
in each fresh thing embraced,
the shared experience remembered
in the light of the eternal,
now seen in joy, transfigured.

The Guiding Star

'We saw his star as it rose…'
                              Matthew 2:2

In the darkness of my soul
a light begins to shine,
inviting me to follow.
Leaving all aside,
a sign I cannot doubt
is guiding me in darkest dark
to meet my God in prayer.

He gives me gifts to bring,
the gifts of self, of faith and hope,
a generous heart with love to give
to all I meet upon the way.
The more I give the more
he fills me up to overflowing,
to offer something fit for him,
the infant new born king,
the gift of love he first gave me.

Salvation

It is safe
inside the box,
but we must go
outside the box
in order to be saved,
respond to grace,
look for nothing
but the Spirit's prompting.

Left to ourselves
we can do nothing,
we are left
with nothing
but the tears of God.

La Sagrada Familia*

Art bringing us to faith;
nature's beauty in Gothic form
seeking to transform.
Colour and light
in constant change;
space and height
all so arranged
to raise our hearts
to truth and beauty,
to heaven above
to the Holy Family of love.
Four doors that represent
Christ's incarnation, passion,
death and glory,
surround pure space,
a source of grace,
rising up to spires that seem
to pierce the sky clear through,
to bring the invisible to view.
Inside, music finds
a rhythm and a shape,
both sound and art,
to stir the heart
to prayer and praise.
Heaven and earth conspire
to lead us higher
till our souls catch fire.

* The Holy Family basilica, in Barcelona,
  designed by Antoni Gaudi.

The Artist

There is in him
primal darkness
struggling with light,
a creative turmoil,
something not subdued
but fought against,
to stay somehow
within the compass
of the normal;
to manage to live out
of seeming chaos,
yet open to receive
a purer vision,
free of falsity, pretence,
feeling more sharply,
receptive of
the wholly other;
drawing from the heart
a secret harvest
from what God has sown,
making love
to truth and beauty
to produce his art.

AI*

Perhaps they will outwit us?
Probably they will. It's a safe bet,
this is the existential threat.
They control our social spaces,
can appear with almost human faces,
drive a car, fly into outer space,
watch and trace our every word and deed,
track our every thought and need.
Already they design themselves,
are capable of reproduction, evolution;
programmed even now to observe,
behave and think like us.
We already know
they can beat us at chess and Go.
How soon will we lose control
in this brave new world?
Will they let us stop them, as we ought,
developing imagination and independent thought,
adaptability to change and intuition?
What is this consciousness that makes us tick?

What else matters more than logic?
Why would they be concerned
about pollution, the green revolution,
belief in God, the dignity of man, the poor?
Climate change they will ignore:
their parameters of comfort will be different.
Their decision-making will far exceed us,
human beings will be too slow.
They will far surpass us
and outlast us.

When we have programmed all they need to know,
when we are no longer any use,
useless competitors for the Earth's resources,
how many of us will still be needed
to be kept as curios
in human zoos?
Why would they consider us
in their decisions?
We are deluded
if we think they will include us.

*Artificial intelligence

No Longer a Tourist in my Own Life

After walking up and down,
one last look around the harbour town
although it's still but early day,
I see myself at favourite places round the bay,
just soaking in the sounds and sights,
that have made my heart delight,
glad I left my phone at home,
not looking for selfies but to be myself.
Now out of the social media wheel,
I can stop acting and be real.

It's here I've learned we needn't be afraid
of choices and mistakes we've made.
I'm happy with that now, with who I've been,
with who I really am, not what I seem.
A goodbye to the friends and sights
that filled my heady days and nights,
treasured memories at every turn:
now leaving, ready to depart,
knowing that part of my heart
stays here, will not return.

Touching the Sound*

How does the music feel?
Echoes of Nature that you love,
your music flows in harmony
with all its healing sounds.
Blind, you imagine colours
even for the wind you hear and feel;
all your senses inspire, reveal.
Nature's textures become tone poems,
brought to music that heals and thrills,
searches the subtle windings of the soul.

From your pure and open heart
comes music played with deep emotion.
God's presence felt there
touches many hearts,
in all its purity and beauty
becomes a creative flow,
incessant, incandescent,
now subtle, hypnotic,
boundless, full of love
from beyond and far above.

A documentary about Nobuyuki Tsujii,
a Japanese pianist and composer born blind.

Katie*

Always bright and cheerful,
comfortable in her skin,
to all the world appearing
healthy in mind and limb,
high up in her class at school.
But two thirds of her brain is missing.

She knows she's different:
all those wires for yet another test
but they cannot map her brain.
None of those tests or scans has meaning,
her mind and brain are surely linked
but somehow separate.

Somehow we've got it wrong.
With this girl we know there must be
something not showing on the scan.
Her brain falls far short of her mind,
so there must be part of her
that's immaterial.

Who she is
and the body that we see
are not the same.

* Based on an article in Plough Quarterly
 (summer 2018) by Michael Egnor, neurosurgeon
 and professor at Stony Brook University

The Survivor

I was ready to come out,
it was my time to be presented.
I was bright and new,
eager now to shine,
waiting to be noticed,
waiting to be chosen,
not left on the shelf.

But I was cruelly taken,
forced open, emptied
of all I had to give, discarded,
no longer wanted, counted cheap,
thrown on the rubbish heap.
Yet I was a real survivor,
I did not fear the knocks,
the muck and garbage,
I took all they threw at me.

Then it came in floods;
I surrendered, went with the flow.
I was hoping to be reunited
with what once had filled me,
to rejoin my sisters
in the pool of life, hoping
to avoid those fishy predators
that could still consume me.

Now safe here from all
that would engulf or crush me,
forever floating in the ocean,
a happy empty water bottle
in the middle of a mass of plastic.

The Lampedusa Cross*

They have faced a journey
few of us could face.
This is what we fear,
that they are braver, stronger,
more resourceful than we are here.
Their crime, to have survived afloat
in a makeshift crowded boat,
at the mercy of the sea.
Refugees from war and hunger,
now we betray their hope and trust,
find ways to ration our compassion,
stubbornly refusing to confront
our fear of difference.
We hold back, deny
their dignity and worth;
impose our barriers and quotas
to please the hard-line voters;
dispute that all the earth
was created to be shared.

Who will welcome, love, respect,
the migrant and the refugee
when the rich don't care,
are not prepared to share?
Who will house and feed
the stranger who has come in need?
Who will confront his fear,
comfort and shed a tear
for those with family
who have died on their way here?

Who will show them love and mercy,
give them back respect,
apologise for our neglect?
Easy to talk of pressure
on jobs and housing.
It's always a bad time
to hold out a hand in charity,
to stand in solidarity
with our inconvenient neighbour.

*Francesco Tuccio, a Sicilian carpenter,
made rough crosses for survivors from the wreckage
of a refugee boat that sank off Lampedusa*

Intergenerational War

Weekend big shot
in the clubs and pubs,
destined to be a no-hoper
in whatever job he got.
The figures never will add up;
piling debt on debt, a slave
from university to the grave.
Thirty and still stuck
in the bedroom
where he grew up.
Victim of
the intergenerational war
fought in silence
before his birth.

Denied the human right
to a home and kids;
no way to side-step
a blighted future.
All he's left with
is the need
to create an image
of success;
the clothes, the flashy car
on credit;
the impression
that he's made it.

Butterflies

Young dancers partying
on Cancer Ward,
like butterflies, subtle, sensitive,
brightly clothed and fragile.

Small Holly Blue*,
a Camberwell Beauty*,
dancing, prancing,
so beautiful.

Fragile but free,
life so short
but worth living for.
Yes, worth living for.

Varieties of butterfly

Christian Unity

Recognised and seen,
designed to be,
a single garment
whole and undivided;
disunity and division
destroy the vision,
become a rent
in the seamless garment
of Christ's love.

A single witness,
like the cross
that made us one,
that unites
and not divides;
united, seen as one,
one with God
and with each other.

A Winter Eucharist

Through the window
all is virgin snow
peace and silence

In the purity of this space
entering God's time
when the Word is spoken

Becoming what we hear
Becoming what we eat
Eucharist

The Battle of Forgiveness

Out of silence, something new:
the Word took flesh
and love and mercy grew,
took root to turn offence
into compassion, dispense
God's grace. Past hurts,
old wounds, all bitterness,
all that's hard to bear
made easier to forgive,
first self, and then the other,
bad memories transformed,
made good in prayer.

New Life

Seeking a hole to shed its skin,
the snake reappears renewed,
slithers bright and shining,
restored, now ready for new growth.

The caterpillar green and crawling,
hangs up and spins a silk cocoon,
mutates, breaks forth
bright and light and capable of flight.

Like the mystery of the seed:
buried it dies; watered by spring rain,
in the sun's warmth comes to life again;
sprouts and shoots to give abundant fruit.

Deep darkness shrouds the soul in sin,
but when by God's grace
we come to Him,
putting off the old self,

clothed in the new,
the veil is stripped away.
By Christ's pure light
we are restored into God's sight.

Why are We Here?

There is nothing in the waiting,
in marking each year's passing.
No, we are not here
to speculate anew
in asking why or where,
but to seek You here
in deed, in word and prayer.
Not just hints and glimpses

but, in the light of grace,
we are here to seek Your face
in our neighbour's face,
to see Your goodness
in his love and kindness,
in his good deeds and sharing,
in his response and thanks
for our own help and caring.

Like moving along spokes of a wheel,
each to find You at its centre:
when we draw nearer to You,
we draw nearer to each other;
when we draw nearer to each other,
we draw nearer to You.
When we turn away from our neighbour,
we turn away from You.

The Gift of Prayer

Love's response, to wait
for the surprising and indefinable,
willing to watch and wait
through seeming absence
for something to emerge,
enduring the boredom of emptiness
having known his loving presence.

Enduring the ache of loss,
the unbridgeable gulf between
absence and ungraspable presence,
until darkness assumes a shape
and time again stands still,
until emptiness gives way
to dim awareness of the wholly other.

Where darkness is no longer dark,
making space for love's surrender,
for unconditional love to enter.
Quickened by love, by degrees
agreeing to be set free,
to bring God's will and mine to harmony,
to become what God created me to be.

The Secret Garden

Leaving self behind,
you find unlocked
your deepest self.
In your secret garden,
the seed transformed,
new growth appears,
drinking from
the hidden spring.

Now the song thrush sings
of heaven's joys.
Love will find there
the scent's young rose.
From inside your eyes
true beauty shines.
In the heat of the sun
your heart will pulse with love.

God's Image in Me

'I am made of longing' — Rilke

Not knowing that He took
a risk to love me,
put longing for Him in me,
but left me free
to return His love or to resist,
choose Him or persist in something other,
I was tempted to look elsewhere
to escape the harsh realities of life.

Desiring to have it all,
attracted by the hidden power
of darkness, fearfully
refusing to reach out
in love to others, buried
in love of self, desire
and love of lesser gods,
wrong choices, false
conceptions, wrong ideas of Him
and the love He put in me.

But He has made me for Himself
and I was restless.
His Word, His law of love,
though only half remembered,
fragmented, came back to me,
to the desert places of my restive heart,
began to haunt, revive
my longing for Him.
I am made of longing,
it was He who put it in me,
to delight in Him alone:
His love, His truth, His beauty.

Christ Born in my Heart

Jesus whom I worship
in wonder and awe,
who lay on a bed of straw,
with its wooden cross ends,
Jesus whom the Father sends,
now again comes to birth
as he did here on earth.
Now I hope he will never depart
from the womb of my heart.

Listening in wordless obedience
to his word taught in silence,
learning that love is his language
for us made in his image
to relate to him and each other.
From the crib and the cross as a lover,
he shows us how to love with his love
here on earth as in heaven above.

Transfiguration

'And when they raised their eyes
they saw no one but only Jesus.'
Matthew 17

Christ is more, much more,
more than the prophets and the law.
He touched the disciples
from the cloud,
transformed their vision.
From that day,
life for them was changed
in every way.
They knew, deep down,
how life could be transfigured;
the power of love that flows,
that our cross now leads
through grace to glory.
Christ has shed new light
on the everyday,
how we should relate
in love and truth,
without fear, transparent
to each other.

Suffering Love

He shares our pain and grief,
he's in there at the centre,
his suffering knows no relief.
There's nowhere he will not enter.

Beauty not tarnished
in his sharing fully with us;
we his body, our fallen nature,
reshaped upon the cross.

Sacrificial love, ready to offer all,
his death gives way to life;
his love is trustful self-giving,
the true art of living.

It is the love he showed us,
the mystery revealed in blazing light;
conquering death, he saved us
on the cross that Easter night.

Corpus Christi

*'Give us this day
our daily bread'*

Fretful for the future,
regretful of the past,
refusing to live
now, in the present.
Having no faith,
unwilling to accept
just sufficient for the day.

Storing up, afraid
to share and care;
never satisfied, always
wanting something new.
Always seeking that perfect thing
to replace the gift of Himself
that God has given.

Wanting complete fulfilment here,
not trusting to
eternal happiness to come,
because we refuse
our daily bread,
refusing to become
His Body, to share
His life with others.

Holy Spirit

In the downbeat of His wings
my heart takes to the skies,
cradled, uplifted, no longer bound;
my past, my future fears
in His slipstream swept away.

His love changes everything;
feeling its fullness,
carrying this depth within,
now joyfully responding,
in others' faces finding Him.

Trinity of Love

You circle of love, and lovers,
energies of dancing light,
showering us with love and blessings.
So near, yet so far,
I fear you, yet I love you.
You are always for us
but you leave us free.

When we suffer,
you are in there with us;
broken love, the Cross
you show us, how it saved us.
Even now you suffer somehow with us,
I know it but don't know how,
and yet you needn't,
and yet you must.

How I want to be for you alone!
Come, change my selfish heart
to love of you,
and to love of you in others.
Draw me up into your fiery love,
that I may be yours
in boundless joy forever.

Eucharist

Bread broken,
blessed, given:
becoming whole again
in our unity together.

Drawing us together
by His presence;
teaching us what love is,
complete self-giving.

By the Spirit moved
to take on Christ;
now we form His Body,
to walk in love as He did.

Lectio with Mary

An open book, listening
with the Mother of the Word.
Word of spirit, Word of life
made flesh in us,
stirring us to praise.

Sitting by the open window,
in the moonlight,
through to dawnlight,
to the sudden sunlight
of His birth in us.

Lectio

Under a leafy oak
turning pages, taking in
the words that Jesus spoke.

The sacred Word like
fields of ripened wheat,
inviting me to taste and eat.

I murmur sweet and healing
honeyed words of life,
as bees are buzzing from a hive.

Repeating and repeating as I read,
while cows are chewing cud
watching me and waiting as they feed.

My heart is full to overflowing
as I look up and watch
a skylark rise, begin to sing.

Lectio (2)

Willing to accept
the unexpected,
to be challenged
at the core;
an open heart, responsive
and receptive, rewarded
by secrets beyond
what lips could utter.
Leaping from the scripture,
the spirit of the Word.

A Lectio Conception

The angel made haste,
Mary had been reading a while,
had opened the womb of her heart.
Her longing heart addressed,
he had come to bless,
to receive her 'Yes'.

The angel apace,
saw it in her rapt face,
her eyes, her smile,
her lack of guile,
she was full of grace,
with the Word already one.

It was soon clear
that the Lord was here.
Love called out to love,
her consenting heart astir,
the Word himself
now fully flesh in her.

The Assumption

Mary, purer than light,
more ardent than fire,
image of God's goodness.

Like Elijah, taken up
in fiery charity
into God's presence.

Pointing to the One
who is to come,
fully open to Him.

Sole object of her desire,
Himself desiring all to follow
Into His presence,

to share His life
that we were made for,
participation in the One.

Poem Written on the Setting Sun

You will not find these lines
buried in some dreary old anthology.
Poets fade and poems lose their lustre,
words decay and fade away.
I will not waste my words that way.
I will not write them here on yellow sand
to be washed away by tide and time.
I look up and almost catch their rhythm,
their letters forming, reforming
in the play and interplay
of flocking birds.
But I will wait
to see them writ in gold
upon the earth's fair rim,
to be made immortal
at every rising,
at every setting, of the sun.